LINCOLI
SERWAI

SEVEN
KEYS

BIBLICAL PRINCIPLES TO
UNLOCK YOUR DESTINY

Foreword by
LARRY TITUS

Published by Eagle's Wings Press

Editing and layout by: EVANGELISTA MEDIA & CONSULTING
Via Maiella, 1 66020 San Giovanni Teatino (CH) – Italy
publisher@evangelistamedia.com
www.evangelistamedia.com

Cover design by: KAIROS CREATIVE
9-11 Cottage Green, London SE5 7ST
info@kairos-media.co.uk
www.kairos-creative.co.uk

For Worldwide Distribution

1 2 3 4 5 6 / 23 22 21 20

DEDICATION

To the womb that bore me, the arms that rocked me, and the lips that first kissed my little face: my loving mother, now in glory, Elizabeth Nakabiri; dearly loved and deeply missed.

ACKNOWLEDGMENTS

I want to thank the brightest shining light in my life, my darling wife, Grace. Where would I even be if I had not found you! You are the most important person to me in every way. Thank you for saying yes when I had nothing, and then walking alongside me passionately, diligently and sacrificially all these years, and raising our amazing sons, Marvin and Jerome.

My brothers, Jimmy and Michael. Do you guys know you feature in most of my dreams? I am beginning to suspect that you have a way of hacking into my nightlife! Thank you for being the most amazing brothers a guy could ever have.

The full-time staff at Liberty Christian Fellowship over the last couple of decades, Pastors Tony, Andrew and Christophe: those hours together every Tuesday morning for months, pouring over God's Word together is one of the main reasons I am still spiritually viable.

Finally, Pastors Amos Kajuga and Hassan Kibirango of Christian Life Assembly in Kigali, Rwanda; remember our conversation at Khana Kazana! Your belief in me was the key to this first offering... and there is more to come! Thanks a million for your love and support. I love you back!

ENDORSEMENTS

The Bible speaks about 'the key of David' in Isaiah 22:22. Some historical commentaries allege that the City of David had a bunch of keys that the king would give to his appointed governor. This bunch of keys was like a 'master key' by which the governor could open the doors to the palace, the temple, the treasury and the armoury. Pastor Lincoln, through this insightful and practical book, has given us the master keys to our God-given territories. By the truths he shares, any locked doors that may confront us in pursuit of our God-ordained path will indeed be flung open as you look out for and apply them.

Michael Kyazze
Senior Pastor, Omega Healing Centre
Director, Omega International Ministries
Kampala, Uganda

I've known Pastor Lincoln for more than three decades. As young men back in Kampala, we sought God together, served together, and struggled together. Even then, Lincoln was a cut above the rest; a born leader. His keen imagination, quick wit and erudite treatment of Scripture has inspired a generation of leaders around the world. His book, *Seven Keys,* unpacks critical elements for any traveller. The takeaways from the stories, along with the pointed applications provide a clear roadmap to success, regardless of your area of calling. Read it. Gift it. It's a must-read!

Dr Dennis D. Sempebwa
President, Eagle's Wings International
CEO, Sahara Wisdom Center
Chancellor, THE 300
Dallas, Texas, USA

Pastor Lincoln Serwanga's book, *Seven Keys,* is as practical and seasoned as the man himself I know. This book is about finding keys to solutions. Solutions to doing things and living a life of purpose. This book will help you find access to obvious and yet subtle struggles of life. It will illuminate your heart and mind so that the dark on your pathway of life today will clear off at your reading and absorbing the gist. The author shares principles that will help you fast-track your life amidst sometimes the obscure junctions, foggy valleys and cloudy hilltops of life.

This book is a must for everyone yearning for godly wisdom in handling issues of life. It will help you embrace your destiny within the parameters of God's Word. Read it; study it; and embrace it. I unreservedly declare with great joy, hope and excitement that this is the book many of us have long been waiting for.

Dr Charles B. Mugisha
Founder and President
Africa New Life Ministries

For over two decades now, Pastor Lincoln Serwanga has been unlocking destinies of many, many people, mainly through Liberty Christian Fellowship in London, but as well as many other spaces globally. It's a passion we share, where he is the teacher. In this wonderful book, *Seven Keys,* he shares both the wisdom and experience that have shaped him into the person, and people builder that he is today. If you are headed anywhere significant, and if you want to take others on this journey, then this book is a must-read. I highly recommend it.

Moses Mukisa
Pastor, Worship Harvest Ministries
CEO, Mo-Mentum Leadership Group

FOREWORD

Lincoln Serwanga answers important questions in this informative and highly inspirational book.

- What is God's plan for my life?

- Will God reveal the plan to me?

- How much of God's plan will He reveal to me?

- How do my talents factor in God's plan?

- What part do others place in my destiny?

- Am I really special or just one of the crowd?

What makes the book so exceptional is how the Bible is foundational to every truth that is revealed. This, coupled with Lincoln's own life-experiences makes the book profound, easily applicable and riveting in its transforming truths. You will come away knowing how special you are in God's economy. Unlike department store garments, where one size fits all, you will learn God has a future for you that is custom designed. You are unique and so is God's design for your life. Since God has been working on this design from eternity, you will find it fits you perfectly.

Larry Titus
President of Kingdom Global Ministries
Apostolic Elder of Waterside Church in Westlake
Dallas, Texas, USA

CONTENTS

PREFACE

Destiny can be difficult to define, let alone pursue. Where does God want me to go? What does He want me to become? What is His plan for my life? These questions can be empowering, or can become overwhelming. Rather than defining destiny as an abstract, invisible, and distant reality, there are day-to-day, step-by-step, and moment-by-moment disciplines and principles, which if you diligently and faithfully attend to, will shape and lead you to your destiny automatically.

Although the word 'destiny' is not found anywhere in Scripture, the principle is clearly taught and implied throughout. God is the God of purpose, not just in redemption but also in creation. God's plan for our individual lives is a finished reality in God and it is ready for us to discover.

In God's commission of Jeremiah the prophet to the difficult task of speaking to the nation of Israel, God assures this reluctant 17-year-old man that there was an ordained path for his life that was determined before his conception:

Then the word of the Lord came to me, saying: "Before I formed you in the womb I knew you; before you were born I sanctified you; I ordained you a prophet to the nations" (Jeremiah 1: 4-5).

In acknowledgment of his sense of a preordained path, King David writes in Psalm 139:16:

Your eyes saw my substance, being yet unformed. And in Your book they all were written, the days fashioned for me, when as yet there were none of them.

Also, in his Epistle to the Ephesians, Paul the apostle points to the reality that God's work in us through Christ is ultimately destined for works that are ordained for us in advance:

For we are his workmanship created in Christ Jesus for good works, which God prepared beforehand that we should walk in them (Ephesians 2:10).

Several years ago, I set my heart to seek God about my path. Other than the painting of the finished picture of my ultimate destination, God began to speak to me about the ingredients of the journey.

I believe this message to be of great significance for every believer to hear. I also know that God put it on my heart that in every church where I am invited to speak for the first time, I should bring this message to that house, unless I am designated a subject or specifically led by God to speak otherwise.

As I sought God, He gave me seven principles that shape the path to our future. In explaining these principles, I will illustrate the principle at work in the scriptural stories of key players in the Bible. I will also testify of my own experience in that specific area. I pray that this journey together will unlock your focus and commitment to observe and apply the truths written here and help lead you to your God-given destiny.

In a nutshell, there are seven keys to unlocking your God-ordained destiny:

1. Key Gifts

2. Key People

3. Key Moments

4. Key Places

5. Key Insights

6. Key Battles

7. Key Choices

As you will see throughout this book, these keys are already at play in your life. Knowing them and how they work will make you better equipped to notice them along your journey. Also, looking back over your life as you read, you may crack a smile or wince a little as you remember the times you applied the keys well and moments when you could have been wiser. Either way, you can now become more intentional as you apply the keys to overcome obstacles and open closed doors.

At the end of each chapter I pose a few questions for you to reflect on and make some decisions. I have no doubt that the stories I tell about my own process will inspire you to remember your own and better plot the way forward.

Chapter 1

KEY GIFTS

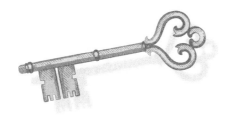

*Pay attention to the gift and the world will
pay attention to you.*

–Nicky Verd

Key gifts are God-given abilities that enable your
unique function on earth in serving His purpose and
meeting needs around you. Deposited at creation, acti-
vated at salvation and enhanced through the Holy Spirit,
this arsenal of abilities is essential in shaping and fulfilling destiny. Your key gifts are like the tool kit of a master
worker. You need to know your tools and how to work

them well to experience fruitfulness, impact your world, and fulfill your God-given assignment.

THE SOUND OF DESTINY

The early 1980s were years of spiritual awakening in Uganda, my country of origin. Every evening of those years was predictable for me, I would be in the company of an exponentially growing crowd of hungry believers clapping, dancing, and enthusiastically singing revival songs in my native language. My whole family and I were brand-new converts to Christ in the wake of the indigenous Pentecostal revival across the country.

Everything dramatically changed for our family when Jesus came home. It was 'Out!' with ancestral worship, the fear of witchcraft, and death—and 'In!' with joy, hope, and hours and hours of prayer, Bible study, and congregating to learn more about this new life. I did not exactly know what lay ahead for me in this war-torn country, but as a high school student with a passion for the sciences and few academic options at the only university in the country, I knew something would take shape by and by.

Quietly walking uphill from home, my shortcut to the church involved going over a fence with the help of a large, God-sent anthill that straddled the iron mesh fence around the church compound. From a fair distance away, the sound of African drums and exuberant singing from the church would drift invitingly to my ears as I approached. This one evening of destiny, as I tumbled down the other side of the anthill into the church compound, an unusual sound caught my ear from around the church house. It was the sound of someone playing a box guitar.

Worship at church in those days was always accompanied by a small ensemble of traditional drums creatively played to diverse rhythms of endlessly looping songs. I played sometimes; but because I was a youth pastor, I was not part of our small dedicated worship team. I am saying all this to explain why the sound of a guitar was such a big surprise and dramatic event for me. I had never physically encountered, let alone heard, the sound of a guitar played live.

Drawn by the sound, my feet followed round the church house until I came upon a group of four familiar faces. A middle-aged brother in the Lord who is now with the Lord, Robert Kyewanula, had brought in a very old box guitar to church and was teaching three young people a song. As I came round upon them, I quickly noted who was there, but my eyes were on one thing, that guitar and the heavenly sound it was making as Robert strummed away with what I later learned was called a plectrum.

Uninvited but captivated, I joined this unscheduled destiny-shaping moment.

That was the first of many times I invited myself along into this little group, and into a new world that helped emerge, define, and launch my key gift that has significantly shaped my destiny. Making music turned out to be a key gift as a singer, musician, and songwriter.

I borrowed that old guitar from Robert after he showed me a few chords and I was firmly on my way. For hours on end, week on week, I strummed away at strings most of which I later learned were not genuine guitar strings, but improvised wires by the owner because he could not afford genuine replacement ones. Soon I was writing songs and holding one-man concerts in front of my family.

DESTINY CALLING

When Moses turned aside to investigate the bush that burned without being consumed, it turned out to be a life-defining moment (Exodus 3:2-4). Small bush fires were probably not uncommon in the wilderness grazing fields; but this bush, in particular, needed investigating because it was not being consumed. I note straightaway that God only called out to Moses when he turned.

I hate to think of what would have happened if Moses had taken a casual look and walked on by. But then again, I believe that God knew Moses well enough; before he started this supernatural bush fire, God knew it would capture his attention as much as He knew the sound of a guitar would capture mine.

Another similar Bible moment was when Mary greeted Elizabeth, the mother of John the Baptist (Luke 1:41). Jesus was the reason for John's conception, and when Mary drew close enough to Elizabeth and greeted her, John leaped inside her womb in recognition of this destiny moment. I like to say that when I heard the sound of the guitar, 'destiny leaped in recognition inside my spirit'. Like Moses, I turned aside to investigate; and like Elizabeth, I began to join the prophetic dots on my Christian call and destiny.

God has such moments for us all, moments that stir up passions and gifts that are placed inside us by God from conception. As you read in the Preface, God tells Jeremiah that his prophetic ordination was before he was formed in the womb (Jeremiah 1:3). The process of discovering and developing these key gifts usually begins as we recognise them at work in others or as we respond to needs around us that begin to awaken them. The faithful use of these gifts then begins to carve out a path and a place for us in this busy, crowded, and competitive world.

Room, Space, and Opportunity

A man's gift makes room for him, and brings him before great men (Proverbs 18:16).

As this proverb shows, it is a man's gift that makes room for him. Relatives, friends, and connections can create opportunities for us, but if we do not have the necessary gifts to occupy the opportunities that they create for us, we shall still have to answer to this principle. It does not even say, 'A man's prayers will make room for him…', and that is not to say prayer is irrelevant to the shaping of our destiny, but when we rise off our knees after praying up a storm, each one of us must express ourselves to the world around us through our gift-set for doors to open. Prayer will create resources, remove obstacles, and open doors. But it's our gifts that pick up from there. So, prayer helps to energise our gifts.

The use of the word 'room' helps us realise that the world is a crowded place with many people stampeding to find a share on the stage of life where opportunities and resources are not always abundant. In the race called life, our gifts are the only way through. Even after finding a place on the stage, the question moves to who is in the audience. According to the promise of this verse, we can capture the attention of 'great men'. When we attend to our gifts and develop them to the utmost, we can climb the ladder of opportunity and end up contributing on the world stage.

YOUR 'KEY' GIFTS

As the word 'key' denotes, you will find that you have several gifts at work in you, but not all of them are key gifts. The idea of a key is the unlocking of doors to access the otherwise restricted space behind them. Some gifts may be helpful in the space but will not grant you access to that space. Also, at different times and seasons, different gifts may be the key.

My musicality, as particularly unlocked through learning to play the guitar, was very key in my young adult stage of life. It was crucial in finding my lifelong friendships, meeting my wife, relocating from Uganda to the United Kingdom, and opening the earliest ministry doors in London. Then my preaching and teaching gift took over in settling me, creating an income, planting a church, and unlocking my international ministry.

I vividly remember the last worship concert we did as a band; as we played the last song that night, these words formed in my mind: 'That's it! I can't do this anymore! I am so hungry to pour myself consistently into a group of people and help them grow spiritually'! From that moment, my key gift expression changed from musician to 'preacher-teacher'. I had been exercising and developing this speaking gift for years, but at this point, it became the lead gift in the unpacking of my ministry journey.

KEY GIFTS IN THE SCRIPTURES

Joseph the Dreamer (Genesis 37–42)

Now Joseph had a dream, and he told it to his brothers; and they hated him even more (Genesis 37:5).

Joseph had the key gifts of dreaming and interpretation of dreams. His destiny as a great deliverer of not just Israel but the whole known world at a time of great famine, was all orchestrated by his dreams, listening to other people's dreams, and knowing the hidden meanings. As a young boy, Joseph's father, Jacob, may have sensed greatness on him, favoured him, and unknowingly but prophetically 'enthroned' him by clothing him with the coat of many colours.

In the beginning, Joseph's gift seemed to just get him into trouble. His brothers hated him for insinuating that they and their father would all one day bow down to him. Their hatred led to an attempt to kill him in the fields before they sold him off to a caravan of Ishmaelites, who in turn sold him in Egypt, the designated place for his destiny and greatness. While working as Potiphar's slave, Joseph was falsely accused by Potiphar's wife of attempted rape and imprisoned. What looked like a series of misfortunes was actually just his pathway to destiny, carved out by the key gift.

While in prison, Joseph accurately interpreted the dreams of the baker and the butler, and that set up the process by which he was brought before Pharaoh, recommended by the butler as a dream interpreter. When he interpreted Pharaoh's dream, Joseph was put in charge of the food strategy he recommended, and was appointed second in command over all Egypt. Years after selling him off to the Ishmaelites, his father and brothers bowed down before him as an Egyptian ruler, just as his dream had shown. Joseph's key gift of dreaming and interpretation made room for him and brought him before great men.

David the Harpist and Warrior

Then one of the servants answered and said, "Look, I have seen a son of Jesse the Bethlehemite, who is skillful in playing, a mighty man of valor, a man of war, prudent in speech, and a handsome person; and the Lord is with him" (1 Samuel 16:18).

David, unlike Joseph, was not loved or favoured by his father, Jesse. Stationed with the sheep, David daily faced the dangers of wilderness shepherding, which involved encounters with lions and bears among other predators. Besides his shepherding tools of rod and staff, David always took a harp with him; and while the sheep grazed and no predator stalked, he would play and recite psalms. When God rejected Saul as king over Israel because of his rebellion, he announced to Samuel the prophet that he had found a man after his own heart. God said, 'Fill your horn with oil, and go; I am sending you to Jesse the Bethlehemite. For I have provided Myself a king among his sons' (1 Samuel 16:1).

When Samuel arrived at Jesse's house, there was nothing to prepare him for what transpired there. He was instructed by God to anoint a smelly, red-faced, 15-year-old shepherd boy, who was brought in from the fields with a harp clutched under his arm. As Samuel walked home, he probably wondered how and when this very private ceremony would translate into a public coronation. The answer, though, was that scruffy harp under David's arm.

Sometime later, Saul, the king, comes under the tormenting influence of a demon spirit and a skilled harpist is sought to relieve him by playing in his presence. That was when David's private devotion to developing his musical gift pays off. One of Saul's servants testifies of David's musical gift and before long, David was standing in the royal palace before the king; his gift has indeed made room for him and brought him before great men. His path from the obscure insignificance of shepherding to the prominence and glory of kingship began with his key gift of playing the harp.

DISCOVER AND DEVELOP YOUR GIFTS

Like Joseph and David, each of us has received key gifts ordained by God to pave the way to our destinies. We need to discover and diligently develop these endowments instead of worrying about our future. In the fulness of time, these gifts will create opportunities and open doors that lead us to our God-given destiny. In a nutshell, God deposits your destiny inside you packaged as passions, gifts, talents, and abilities that if fully expressed will unfold the plan of God for your life.

A PERSONAL STORY:
FROM MUSICIAN TO PASTOR

As I testified at the beginning of this chapter, my encounter with the guitar started for me a journey into discovering and developing my key gift as a musician.

Regrettably, there were huge limitations in my environment that meant my skills as a guitarist, songwriter, and vocalist could not rise as high as I would have desired. But by being faithful to what I had, God graciously led me to key people as I will show later in this story. Key people led me to other key people, key moments, and key places. As I write this book today, I am a lead pastor of a church in London and travelling quite widely as a conference speaker. The path that brought me here I can trace significantly back to that moment when 'the baby leaped within me' at the sound of a guitar. This is the perfect illustration of the principle of key gifts at work.

APPLICATION

As we close the discussion on key gifts, I want to share my understanding of the various types of gifts, and even talents and skills to help you do a personal audit.

I believe our bank of gifts falls into three different categories: 1) Gifts of Father God; 2) Gifts of the Son; 3) Gifts of the Holy Spirit. Let's look at each of these closely.

1. Gifts of Father God

These are abilities deposited by God at creation within each individual. They are not acquired—they are discovered. These gifts need cultivation and development to reach their full potential, and the ability lies inside each of us, waiting to be discovered.

I believe these gifts of Father God fall into two broad categories: 1) Personality Profiles and 2) Natural, Latent Talents.

- Personality Profiles. These are also called temperaments. Popular tools used in profiling include the Myers-Briggs Type Indicator Test, and the Hartman Personality Profile. There may be a degree to which temperaments are affected by upbringing and life experiences, but at the core, personality diversities are God-ordained and provide a foundational base from which skills and talents can be cultivated. Because of the fall of humankind, these personality types will exhibit negative characteristics that have to be dealt with—but that does not negate God's original purpose in creating one person who is an extrovert and another an introvert, or one emotionally intense and another quite laid back. I strongly recommend you take these tests for yourself to develop a clear sense of your personality profile. You can also look into Working Style tests, as well as the well-known Love Languages by Gary Chapman.

- Natural, Latent Talents. These are talents to which you are naturally inclined including art, social, technical, music, mathematics, etc.

When you are naturally gifted by God in a particular field, you will find picking up and developing various skills in that field very easy while others struggle to get ahead.

2. Gifts of the Son

These gifts are seen in Paul's epistle, Ephesians, and attributed to Christ and His ascension:

> *Therefore He says, "When He ascended on high, He led captivity captive, and gave gifts to men." Now this, "He ascended"—what does it mean but that He also first descended into the lower parts of the earth? He who descended is also the One who ascended far above all the heavens, that He might fill all things.) And He Himself gave some to be apostles, some prophets, some evangelists, and some pastors and teachers* (Ephesians 4:8-11).

Although these gifts have traditionally been described as being specifically given to anointed, front-standing ministers in the body of Christ, it is popularly believed that the list also points to a fivefold enabling of the whole body:

- Apostolic – strategic; entrepreneurial people.

- Prophetic – inspirational; creative and artistic people.

- Evangelistic – befriending; attraction and persuading people.

- Pastoral – caring; nurturing and shepherding people.

- Teacher – instructional; truth-driven people.

3. Gifts of the Spirit

In 1 Corinthians 12:7-11, Paul the apostle describes nine different manifestations of the Holy Spirit that have been popularly divided into utterance, revelation, and power gifts as follows:

- Utterance gifts: diversities of tongues, interpretation of tongues and prophecy.

- Revelation gifts: words of knowledge, words of wisdom, discernment of spirits.

- Power gifts: gift of faith, gifts of healing, and working of miracles.

In light of your understanding of the three types of gifts, please complete the following profiling questions:

1. **What are your Father God gifts?**

    - What is your Myers-Briggs personality profile score?

    - What is your Hartman personality profile score?

    - What is your Working Style?

    - What are your Love Languages?

    - What are your natural skills, tendency, and talents?

2. **What are your Son gifts? (Usually, we tend to carry two of these five gifts.)**

    ☐   Apostolic

    ☐   Prophetic

    ☐   Evangelistic

    ☐   Pastoral

    ☐   Teacher

3. What are your Spirit gifts? (I believe that you can grow in seeing all these gifts working through you, but you will still find a handful of them expressing more readily.)

☐ Tongues

☐ Interpretation of tongues

☐ Prophecy

☐ Word of knowledge

☐ Word of wisdom

☐ Discernment of spirits

☐ Gift of Faith

☐ Gifts of Healing

☐ Working of Miracles

CHAPTER 2

KEY PEOPLE

I meet people and they become
chapters in my stories.

—Avijeet Das

Our lives are shaped by key people. Starting with our family upbringing, relatives and friends, workmates and spouses, and even complete strangers—defining moments both good and bad happen to us throughout life. If surrendered and properly processed with God, these will work together to lead us into our destiny.

A Friend Closer than a Brother

My first encounter with my now best friend still glows brightly in my memory. I was a freshman in the Agriculture programme at Makerere University, Kampala (MUK). MUK was the only university in Uganda in those days, and to have made my way there was a great opportunity to meet some of the best minds and hearts from the whole country.

As a naturally shy and introverted young person, I had not made many friends growing up. The few friendships I remember having were very extroverted individuals who had somehow noticed my isolated state, walked up to me, and invited me to their group of followers. I fondly remember these gregarious, dominant characters in primary, secondary and high school days. My university experiences though were to be even more memorable because of them.

Bright-eyed, round-faced, fun-loving, and easy-going, my best friend, whose name I have chosen to leave out, was one of the gravitating points of the whole university class. Everybody was his friend! And that was not because of a choice we made. This wonderful man invited himself into our space and our world. We were all swept along by his storm of friendly chats, witty humour, easy manner, and fearless friendliness. I just could not quite understand how he did it. The great thing was that he was a committed Christian like me, and musical as well, a player of keyboards. Soon we became special friends because of our shared faith and love of music.

In our second year, we shared a room at the university farm and became members together of a revival and worship awakening band named Restoration, performing in missions' programmes in schools, colleges, churches, and more. In this environment of intense connection and interaction, I learned how extroverted living looked like from the front row of watching him crash into people's lives and befriend them all—men, women, old and young, students and lecturers alike. I remember making it my intention to observe him doing his thing: to look, listen, learn, and imitate him. It was mainly because of him that my mostly silent, isolated, introverted manner thawed into a more sociable, friendly one. He was a key person in the shaping of my relational and leadership gift.

From university days to today, this special man remains to me 'a friend…closer than a brother' (Proverbs 18:24). His love and support has added value to my life and ministry beyond calculation. If I was to 'select all' and 'delete' his influence from my life, I would in that instant end up elsewhere, poorer, less impactful, and less fruitful.

I will mention other names in this book who even though not under the banner of 'key people' were key players in the writing of the journey to where I am today. In the previous chapter, I may have eclipsed Robert Kyewanula behind the guitar that he played and later taught me to play, but he was a key person too. As you read this now, your mind must be lighting up with the faces of multiple key people who have impacted your life. Whether the impact was good or evil, all can still work out for good in the shaping of who you become for God.

RUTH, NAOMI, AND BOAZ

But Ruth said: "Entreat me not to leave you, or to turn back from following after you; for wherever you go, I will go; and wherever you lodge, I will lodge; your people shall be my people, and your God, my God. Where you die, I will die, and there will I be buried. The Lord do so to me, and more also, if anything but death parts you and me" (Ruth 1:16-17).

A most regrettable association opens up the book of Ruth. Three widows together was not exactly a good team in ancient Israel. Women had no rights or identity on their own in those days, and widows even worse. Naomi's two sons had both died and their young wives were now stuck with her. Naomi does the honourable thing and releases them to move on and find a better life for themselves.

Orpah, one of the young women, gladly complies with Naomi's plea and leaves. She not only leaves Ruth but walks right off the pages of Scripture and is never heard of again. Ruth, whose name becomes the title of this Bible book, refuses to go. Instead, she makes a covenant commitment to Naomi, the intensity of which is borrowed by countless Christian couples as a reading in marriage services worldwide. Somehow, although Naomi looks resourceless and helpless, Ruth perceives that she is a key person to her. She pledges to stay with Naomi to the point of death and burial.

Covenant Commitment

I really would have loved to watch the expression on Naomi's face that day in response to such a passionate vow. We all would love to have people in our lives who so believe in who we are and what we carry that they commit to us even when nothing is going for us. That is one way to define key people; people who see more in you than meets the eye and make a silent vow to be there with you for better or worse. Spouses, lifelong friends, mentors, even proteges, and key family members should ideally all answer to this definition. Occasionally, even heartbreakers can play a key role if we take our pain to God and allow Him to mould us through it all.

As the story of Ruth unfolds, she is married to Boaz to whom the duty of marrying her fell in the tradition of 'kinsmen redeemers'. According to Levitical law, the brother of a deceased man was obligated to marry his widow and take care of her (Deuteronomy 25:5). This was not always done, as we can see from Boaz's own reluctance in the story. But out of it, Ruth conceives, and her son Obed forms a key link in the genealogy of Christ through Joseph (Matthew 1:1-16). Ruth's commitment to Naomi as a key person writes her name firmly into the very genealogy of the Messiah.

There are many more key people stories we can learn from in the Scriptures. Let's look at a few of them.

SAUL MEETS SAMUEL THE PROPHET (MENTORS)

In the book of 1 Samuel, Saul the son of Kish leaves home, sent by his father to look for lost donkeys—and he comes back home anointed king of Israel. Instead of finding the lost animals, Saul met a key person in Samuel the prophet. As the story goes, God was involved in the escape of the donkeys to get Saul out of his father's house on an otherwise frustrating mission in itself. The day before, God had said to the prophet:

> *"Tomorrow about this time I will send you a man from the land of Benjamin, and you shall anoint him commander over My people Israel, that he may save My people from the hand of the Philistines; for I have looked upon My people, because their cry has come to Me"* (1 Samuel 9:16).

Unexpected and unscheduled, this encounter with Samuel completely altered the trajectory of Saul's life and made him the first-ever man to sit on the throne of Israel. We know that he squandered the opportunity to establish his throne generationally through disobedience, but the point still stands, that his destiny was shaped by encountering a key person. The story also points to the power of a mentor in impacting your life through instruction, prophetic ministry, and spiritual impartation.

DAVID MEETS JONATHAN (FRIENDS AND PEERS)

One of life's greatest and quite rare gifts is finding a covenant friend. One such tale is that of David and Jonathan, the son of Saul the king. In line to succeed his father on the throne of Israel, Jonathan meets David because of his presence in the royal courts, as a servant of Saul. Somewhere in the course of their acquaintance, a miracle of the heart happens and is captured in the Scriptures:

> *Now when he had finished speaking to Saul, the soul of Jonathan was knit to the soul of David, and Jonathan loved him as his own soul. Saul took him that day, and would not let him go home to his father's house anymore. Then Jonathan and David made a covenant, because he loved him as his own soul. And Jonathan took off the robe that was on him and gave it to David, with his armor, even to his sword and his bow and his belt* (1 Samuel 18:1-4).

In what seems to be a moment of instant bonding, Jonathan's heart knits to David's through what should have been spontaneous recognition of him as a key person for him. Then in a shocking act of complete selflessness, Jonathan virtually surrenders his right to the throne to David by giving him his robe and his whole armour. Several times after this moment, Jonathan secretly informed David of his own father's murderous plots against him and helped David escape.

Just like Jonathan, there are key people along the path of our lives, ordained by God to come to our rescue and service. They will advise, warn, and make sacrifices for us as brothers, sisters, and friends only would.

JESUS AND THE TWELVE DISCIPLES (PROTEGES)

Now it came to pass in those days that He went out to the mountain to pray, and continued all night in prayer to God. And when it was day, He called His disciples to Himself; and from them He chose twelve whom He also named apostles... (Luke 6:12-16).

Early in His earthly mission, Jesus prayed all night in preparation for a key moment. He knew that His time on earth was limited and that He would hand over His mission to a team of proteges to continue His work. It was not a small decision, and He invests in prayer all night to His Father enquiring and listening. By daybreak, Jesus' mind is clear on the way forward and He calls His disciples to Himself and chooses twelve key people. For the rest of His time on earth, He pours Himself into these men and ultimately turns over the mission to them. Interestingly, one of the disciples is Judas who later betrays Jesus: he was a key person too, a key to the shaping of Jesus' destiny.

The lessons out of this story are clear. Firstly, we need to understand that our destiny is not only shaped by those who deposit into our lives, but also by those into whose lives we pour. We need to prayerfully seek God's face to lead us to the people He wants us to devote ourselves to by coaching, training, and mentoring them. Instructing others is vitally important to our own growth because we understand what we know even better when we pass it on to others. Also, leading others exposes us to areas of personal development that no other way can.

A Personal Story: Finding My Wife, Grace

One evening as a freshman at university campus, on the steps of St. Francis, the university chapel, I spoke to this passionate, beautiful girl for the first time after a Christian Union meeting. I did not know I was looking into the eyes of the future mother of my children, my life companion, and the best thing that ever happened to me. Over the months that followed, we had more conversations after the meetings. I also visited her at her hall of residence. She was part of Restoration Band. Our passion for the supernatural, hours of band practice, extended worship and prayer together, and serving God made us a close-knit family of brothers and sisters. These friends became key people and lifelong friends.

Part of my Christian commitment at conversion was a defining, unspoken vow by which I separated myself from defiling relationships with girls. As a band, we enjoyed the company of five lovely young women who were each passionately in love with Jesus and committed to us as their brothers. But then there was Grace; I seemed to connect with her in ways I did not know how to explain. Many times on our missions, in the unpredictable moments that awaited us beyond what we could prepare for, I somehow always felt connected and oriented through her collaboration. Our bond spiritually and emotionally developed very effortlessly.

Then one day, I woke up to a realisation, as I will share more on this story in the chapter on Key Moments. To me, it was all about God's timing. Let me keep you guessing and wrap this up by saying that today we have two amazing grown-up sons and continue to serve God side by side. And again, if I was to 'select all' and 'delete' this beautiful woman's love, partnership, and voice of influence from my life, you would not be reading this book, there would be no Liberty Christian Fellowship in London, and I am quite sure I would have self-destructed. She is not just the path to my destiny, she is the summary of it.

APPLICATION

In this application, take a moment to look back over your life and identify key people who have significantly impacted your life. This can also be a good moment to convert negative experiences into capital for your journey to destiny. That would mean forgiving offenders and representing those experiences to yourself in redemptive ways.

1. Who have been your most significant key people so far, and how have they helped shape your destiny? Is there a need for you to renew some of these connections?

2. What relational events have negatively impacted you in the past? Is there still a need to forgive, release, and make these memories work for your benefit? What does God want you to take away

from these memories as a propulsion towards your destiny?

3. Who are your current and emerging key people and what role are they playing?

4. Are you aware of your covenant relationships thus far? Do the people know that they are that important to you? Consider having conversations with them and being honest about how you see their place in your life and journey.

5. Who has God strategically committed to your care for your growth and development? Are you being faithful in serving and discipling them? Make a fresh commitment to these relationships going forward.

Chapter 3

KEY MOMENTS

So much of life is not about whether you're good or bad, or right or wrong, or can afford or not afford—it's just about timing.

—A. A. Gill

Our lives are shaped by moments. From the time we are born, for the rest of our lives, we walk through life in search of key moments. It is in these moments the rest of the principles in this book are nested. As an old saying goes, 'Time is God's way of not letting everything happen at once'. Key moments are God's way of writing the story of your life one chapter at a time.

In March 1987, my heart and mind suddenly came to attention about an area I had put aside from the time of my conversion as a 19-year-old: it was time to find my wife! It felt like a spiritual awakening and activation. This is not to say that I did not have an awareness of this area or of the presence of fine, godly young women all around me during these strategic university years. I just had no witness or engagement in my spirit about it. But now, in a moment as clear as the difference between night and day, I felt suddenly authorised from the deepest part of my being to resolve this area; this was a key moment.

As I explained in the preceding chapter, there already were five very significant and God-fearing women around me and close to me relationally. But to me, that was not necessarily the point. In my heart, I was completely surrendered to God's will in this area, whatever that looked like. On this day as I awoke to this intense urge from the Lord, I renewed my surrender to His will. But even as I did that, I felt a creeping thought grafting into the end of my prayer of surrender: 'Not my will, but Your will be done, Lord...but she better be like Grace'!

Over the months and years of waiting for God and interacting with womankind, an outline had been forming inwardly of what true companionship feels and looks like. And now at this key moment, it was impossible to be blinded by mere beauty, status, or anything else.

I had a sense that until this inner work was done, there was no map within me to help form a clear witness.

So for me at this key moment, the outline was clear and had a name—that name was Grace Kalimuzo. After several weeks of praying, listening, and seeking the witness of some key people around me, I came to another key moment: I felt God say to me, 'Today you must speak with her and ask her to marry you'. It was strong and it was clear. He also said to me, 'She is at her friend's place, Jennifer, in Mulago. Go and speak to her there'.

Now, it's not that I hear God that clearly every day, but at key moments over very important areas of our lives, there will be so much grace and activation that we will hear God clearer than at other times if we choose to seek and listen. So I dressed up decently and made the fairly short trek to Mulago. As I got to the house and looked in through the open front door, there she was! To me, that was the final witness on this path to my destiny. After some time chatting and laughing together, I asked Jennifer if I could speak to Grace privately.

I did not pull out an engagement ring or recite a scripted speech. I do not remember verbatim what I said exactly, but I had a clear sense that she knew that we belonged together. I told her that I had prayed and sought advice and witness about what I was about to tell her. Then I asked if she felt, like I did, that we belong together—forever.

She did! Then I found out that she had known from the Lord about me for a couple of years already and was just waiting for it to be confirmed and fulfilled.

At some point, I remember that Jennifer interrupted our private conversation by running into the room with a bunch of flowers she had hastily picked from around the compound, smiling cheekily from ear to ear. Unknown to me, she and Jennifer were just talking about it all before I showed up at the door. That day the three of us walked together to our band practice and it felt like I was walking on clouds! It was a day like none ever before; a key gift had led me to a key person, at this very key moment.

A TIME FOR EVERYTHING

I returned and saw under the sun that—the race is not to the swift, nor the battle to the strong, nor bread to the wise, nor riches to men of under-standing, nor favor to men of skill; but time and chance happen to them all. For man also does not know his time: like fish taken in a cruel net, like birds caught in a snare, so the sons of men are snared in an evil time, when it falls suddenly upon them (Ecclesiastes 9:11-12).

As these verses from Ecclesiastes 9 show, there is a time for everything in our lives. When it comes to it, just being swift, wise, strong, understanding, or even favoured in itself, will lead nowhere if the timing is wrong. You may get very busy, but nothing of real consequence in terms of building towards your destiny will happen. These virtues all work well when they are synchronised with the right timing. Sometimes it is not possible to know the correct moment. But when you know there is such a thing as a key moment, it helps you to at least keep praying, keep waiting, keep believing, and keep trying without getting discouraged.

A business article I read some time ago left me fascinated. In the world of business start-ups, research has shown that it is not actually how good your business idea is, or how much capital you have, or how good your strategy, business model, or team is—the most important factor for business success is actually timing. Nothing can get in the way of an idea whose time has come.

Timing Determines Navigation

When using a route-finder such as Google Maps to get to a destination, the GPS calibrates your journey in terms of distance and time to each manoeuvre. The audio instructions sound something like, 'In twenty-five meters turn left' or, 'In approximately five minutes turn right'. If you turn too early or too late, you will be going the wrong direction and the algorithm will recalculate to bring you back on course. I remember a couple of times when I intentionally kept driving farther and farther away from the intended destination, defying the GPS audio prompting each time just to see what it would ultimately do. I came to a point where the navigation recalculation and prompting stopped altogether. I guess beyond a certain point the route-finder was programmed to just stop prompting. I had to pull over and re-enter the destination before the app resumed directions for my route.

In the same way, God will only redirect us if we stop disregarding His voice at key moments. I found that when you keep disobeying, His voice and your witness of God becomes dimmer and dimmer to the point of no longer hearing what He is saying. But if you stop and recommit to His will, however far you may be from God's original will for you, He will redirect you back to your right destination.

OTHER SCRIPTURES ABOUT KEY MOMENTS

God's Timing

We then, as workers together with Him also plead with you not to receive the grace of God in vain.

For He says: "In an acceptable time I have heard you, and in the day of salvation I have helped you." Behold, now is the accepted time; behold, now is the day of salvation (2 Corinthians 6:1-2).

As this Scripture passage vividly shows, the grace of God works very much within God's timing. To miss His timing is to miss His grace for the moment. When we try to do things outside of God's window of time, we will find that there is no divine enablement or favour to release the expected results.

Times of Harvest

• *Sowing and Reaping*

Those who sow in tears shall reap in joy. He who continually goes forth weeping, bearing seed for sowing, shall doubtless come again with rejoicing, bringing his sheaves with him (Psalm 126:5-6).

These two verses show that there are times ordained by God for us to reap the harvest in areas where we have sown diligently and patiently. If we miss the time of sowing, there will not be a time of harvest.

- *Exceptional Harvest*

"Behold, the days are coming," says the LORD, *"when the plowman shall overtake the reaper, and the treader of grapes him that sows seed; the mountains shall drip with sweet wine, and all the hills shall flow with it* (Amos 9:13).

In this verse, God sows His rule over our times and seasons by which He can sovereignly collapse the waiting time, and cause seed time and harvest to coincide at key moments. The same idea is shown in the following Scripture.

- *Times of Restoring Lost Harvest*

Be glad then, you children of Zion, and rejoice in the Lord your God; for He has given you the former rain faithfully, and He will cause the rain to come down for you—the former rain, and the latter rain in the first month. The threshing floors shall be full of wheat, and the vats shall overflow with new wine and oil. So I will restore to you the years that the swarming locust has eaten, the crawling locust, the consuming locust, and the chewing locust, My great army which I sent among you. You shall eat in plenty and be satis-fied, and praise the name of the Lord your God, who has dealt wondrously with you; and My people shall never be put to shame (Joel 2:23-26).

Personal Story: Leasing Our Church Venue

In 2009, our church finally found and occupied our current building in South London on a twenty-five-year lease agreement. Everything in the process of securing it worked on timing.

Before this building, we had found another premises and had completed all negotiations and waited to officially sign the lease documents. On the day that we were due to sign, I received a telephone call from our new landlord. In an unexplained change of mind, he announced to me that he was not going through with the arrangement. The news was devastating because the church already celebrated this breakthrough and were anticipating the move.

A few months later, I received a call from one of our lay leaders who had just been placed in charge of evangelism and church growth. For her, finding a building had become a priority, because in her reasoning, a church cannot really grow unless it had a secure base. So she set off on a premises-hunting campaign.

'I have found a building in Camberwell'! she announced to me. 'You must see it straight away!' I did not know what to think. Empty buildings to lease were hard to come by in London and continue to be so. That aside, landlords were increasingly inclined against churches, and for every building that came onto the market, there was always a stampede, as churches rushed to get ahead of each other. She had already organised a viewing appointment, so I scheduled to be present and made my way to view the site.

When I arrived, the property agent was standing with the landlord outside the building. The landlord was a Sikh Indian man, turban on head, grey beard, with his S Class Mercedes parked in front of the building. As you can imagine, the first few seconds of this encounter were nerve-racking. Would this Sikh landlord have any willingness to support our occupancy as a church? I shook his hand and then the agent's nervously. Then the agent's mobile phone rang, and he excused himself to take the call; that interruption turned out to be a key moment.

While the agent spoke on the phone, possibly agreeing with another church on their way to view the building, I turned to the landlord and began to discuss our need for the building. In those few moments, this dignified man, most probably in his 60s made statements I was desperate to hear, 'I am ok for you to use this as a church. If you look at the building and like it, you can have it'!

Then nodding discreetly towards the agent on the phone, he continued. 'We can forget about him and you deal directly with me. Come to my office with some money to show me you are serious, and I will give you the keys'.

In that key moment lasting only a few moments, any other tenants hoping to get the building were closed out. After viewing the building and then taking our architect along to have a look, we agreed to move forward and went to the owner's offices with a securing deposit. During the surreal conversation that transpired there, money changed hands and so did keys to the building. We have been worshiping and ministering from that very building to the time I am writing these words. After years of searching desperately for a favourable landlord and a suitable building, both came through an unbelievable key moment.

APPLICATION

1. Think back and acknowledge the key moments of your journey so far. What happened and what did God teach you then?

2. In what season are you currently, and what is God saying to you now?

3. What doors are you waiting on God to open? Are there any changes in your thinking and behaviour that you believe could accelerate your journey?

CHAPTER 4

KEY PLACES

*Keep your eyes open and your feet moving
forward. You'll find what you need.*

—Anonymous

Time always works with space and matter to deliver
the bullet points of our story. When space and matter
combine, we find locations on this earth that become the
addresses for our transformative encounters. Many times
in Scripture, God used specific venues for His orchestrated
events to happen. Being at the right place at the right time
is essential to the moulding of our lives in Christ and the
shaping of our destinies.

Many times there is a geographical element to the release of God's blessing. God is the God of locations and addresses.

A Personal Story: Buying Our Family Home

I am typing these words from the comfort of my home in Anerley, South London. My family occupied this property about nineteen years ago as a brand-new building through a special scheme enabling young families in the UK to purchase a home in stages. From the time when Grace and I were married in 1989, we had moved to five different rental homes, still unable to purchase a home. Most of our tenancies did not last more than two years, and the disruption of being asked by the landlord to move was unbearable each time, as furniture is damaged and life disrupted by the process. As relatively fresh immigrants, we were still unable to save sufficiently for a deposit to buy a home...until I received a call from California, USA.

The call was from a good friend from the earliest months of my conversion to Christ. We met at church as young people and connected through a mutual love for extended prayer and a hunger to see God touch our generation. Then at some point after university, he emigrated to the USA on a ministry mission. After powerful and extensive ministry up and down the USA, he married and settled his young family in Los Angeles, where he was in the first stages of church planting from his living room. He was now inviting me to visit him, meet his family, and perhaps connect with some of his pastor friends and hopefully even preach my first sermon in America.

A little reluctantly, I accepted the invitation and purchased my ticket on my credit card. After two weeks in the Golden State and the City of Angels, I returned to London with a ticket debt to clear and having preached in two churches in LA: one being my friend's nucleus church comprised of him, his wife and daughter, and two members; the other a tiny Nigerian church plant with about ten members! That was my first experience of ministry in the USA. But then something else happened while I was in LA; one of my other friends living in Seattle, Washington, invited me to fly through there on my way home.

My friend in Seattle is another of my key people, a lifelong friend from university days, and one of the five men in the Restoration Band. I flew to Seattle and had a blast of a time reconnecting with him and meeting his wife and family. Seattle was a key place for me in this story.

A week after returning home, definitely buoyed and inspired by my trip to the US, I received a call from Seattle. Prayerfully, my friend and his wife had decided to send

Grace and me money to support us as we continued in our mission here. My jaw dropped as he told me the amount. Those two small churches I visited could not do much to bless me, but what mattered to God was that I stepped out and went where He wanted me to go.

A few months on, my family moved into a 3-bedroom house that we were able to part-purchase through the gift sent from Seattle! It was near the exact amount needed for the deposit on our mortgage.

STUMBLING INTO KEY PLACES

Now Jacob went out from Beersheba and went toward Haran. So he came to a certain place and stayed there all night, because the sun had set. And he took one of the stones of that place and put it at his head, and he lay down in that place to sleep. Then he dreamed, and behold, a ladder was set up on the earth, and its top reached to heaven; and there the angels of God were ascending and descending on it. And behold, the Lord stood above it and said: "I am the Lord God of Abraham your father and the God of Isaac; the land on which you lie I will give to you and your descendants. Also your descendants shall be as the dust of the earth; you shall spread abroad to the west and the east, to the north and the south; and in you and in your seed all the families of the earth shall be blessed. Behold, I am with you and will keep you wherever you go, and will bring you back to this land; for I will not leave you until I have done what I have spoken to you" (Genesis 28:10-15).

In the story above, Jacob was fleeing from his enraged bother Esau, after impersonating him before his blinded father Isaac, and stealing his blessing (Genesis 27:1-29). For the first time in his life, he experiences an encounter with the God of his father and grandfather for himself while resting his head on a stone in a completely random location. This place, Bethel, becomes a key reference point in Jacob's life and destiny. God even later identifies Himself to Jacob saying, 'I am the God of Bethel, where you anointed the pillar and where you made a vow to Me' (Genesis 31:13).

For the first time, Jacob hears the affirming voice of the God whose blessing and promises he had so desired that he had got himself into the situation of having to flee for his life. What he recognises immediately from what God spoke to him was that his destiny as a person was tied to the location where he was standing right there. 'How awesome is this place. This is none other than the house of God, and this is the gate of heaven'! (Genesis 28:16-17).

Although his life was in upheaval at this point, Jacob took the time to stop, anoint a stone and make vows to God at this key place. Like him, it is important that we stop long enough to acknowledge the key places that God leads us to whether we planned our way there or just stumbled upon them.

At key geographical locations that we come to, God's plans and purposes will suddenly accelerate because they are geo-tagged to these locations. Such places include countries, regions, churches, workplaces, and the like. The point may not be merely in the physical spaces. I am not trying to advocate for a veneration of objects or mere physical locations but a stewardship of memorials and the honouring of the lessons, relationships and blessings that have come to us through specific places. We need to take note of the people and the unique needs, opportunities, and dynamics connected to these locations. It is, therefore, important to realise that the pursuit of destiny must involve for us a willingness to move or travel to locations by God's leading and make the necessary commitments necessary to these key places.

OUR VISIT TO ISRAEL

Several years ago, our church sponsored my wife and I for a trip to Israel. We visited multiple sites that we have always read about in the Bible. It was an eternally memorable experience. Standing on the very ground and entering the spaces where the patriarchs, kings, prophets and even Jesus Himself once stood was incredibly inspiring.

As our tour guide narrated the various Bible stories in the very location of their historical occurrence, these events seemed to come immediately alive in my heart as if they were happening right then. Specifically, as we walked in the shepherds' field where the choir of angels are known to have appeared to the shepherds by night, I seemed to even hear them sing still. And then there was the empty tomb at the place of the skull where Jesus is believed to have been laid for the three days before His glorious resurrection. These are key places that every believer needs to visit if possible and just experience the memorials of the Bible stories. Of course, every pilgrim there will have a different experience. One thing for sure is you will realise the importance of places and their memorials in your journey with God.

OTHER BIBLE VERSES ON KEY PLACES

- ## *Elijah at the Brook Cherith*

Then the word of the LORD came to him [Elijah], saying, "Get away from here and turn eastward, and hide by the Brook Cherith, which flows into the Jordan. And it will be that you shall drink from the brook, and I have commanded the ravens to feed you there" (1 Kings 17:2).

After pronouncing a drought over all Israel, Elijah's survival through the dearth that followed was subject to him going to and staying at a specified location as instructed by God. Ravens, which are notorious for not sharing their food, were instructed by God to take food to Elijah at the Brook Cherith. If he had gone anywhere else, it would have seemed like God had failed to provide for him. But there, he drank from the brook and the ravens faithfully fed him. Later after the brook had dried up, God relocated Elijah to the home of a widow where the form of provision changes from ravens' delivery to the multiplication of the widow's food (1 Kings 17:7-16). We can count on God to provide for us at the locations where He sends us.

• *The Call of Abraham*

Now the Lord had said to Abram: "Get out of your country, from your family and from your father's house, to a land that I will show you. I will make you a great nation; I will bless you and make your name great; and you shall be a blessing. I will bless those who bless you, and I will curse him who curses you; and in you all the families of the earth shall be blessed" (Genesis 12:1-3).

The call and blessing of Abraham was conditional on him uprooting himself from the relative comfort of the Ur of the Chaldeans, and taking on a life pitching his tent around a fairly hostile region, in pursuit of an uncertain destination. As he adopted this nomadic lifestyle, God opened his wife Sarah's womb and brought forth Isaac, his child of promise.

MEMORIES VERSUS DESTINY

Like Abraham our father of faith, we need to commit ourselves to pilgrimage through life in surrender to God's will. It is so easy to get sentimentally attached to locations that have many precious memories. But God has not called us to the mere creation of memories but also the stewardship of destiny. Uprooting ourselves from comfort zones as well as having the grace and courage to let people move on when they must, is central to understanding that key places may change.

MISSION TO LONDON

At the end of my university course, I was getting packed to vacate my room at the university hall where I had completed my fourth year of study when I heard a knock at the door.

As the door opened, a key person stepped into the room. This prophetic man was a good friend, the out-going leader of the University Christian Union and in the same hall of residence as me. He had a clear and strong prophetic reputation. He asked for a moment to tell me what God had shown him the night before.

'I did not sleep much last night', he started. His blood-shot eyes bore clear witness to that truth. 'I was praying for you last night, and God gave me a word for you'. I sat up keen to hear the rest. 'God will take you out of this country to another country; and while there, He will raise you up as a leader in the revival and what He wants to bring there. God will bless you there and prosper you if you serve Him faithfully'. After a short prayer during which I wondered how in the world these things would happen, he bid farewell and left.

Several months later, our band, Restoration, received an invitation to come to London for a short ministry course at Kensington Temple, in West London. As we prayed about this invitation, not everyone in the band felt a witness to go; for various reasons, Grace, who was my fiancée at that time, and one other group member who has since gone to be with the Lord, and I had a clear sense to accept the invitation on the first opportunity. We would do the course and the others would probably join us to minister and also raise some sponsorship for our mission around Uganda and Africa.

In August 1988, we landed at Gatwick airport and got a six-month visitor visa at UK immigration. That was thirty-two years ago, and we are still here. On March 18, 1989, Grace and I were married at Kensington Temple and two years later we planted Liberty Christian Fellowship. I thank God that Grace and I responded obediently to this call to relocate. The personal cost for us has been enormous on many fronts, but it is clear that London UK is God's key place for us.

That prophetic word about relocating to another country has been fulfilled, and we continue to believe and wait for the spiritual awakening that God promised. I know that the voice that God has made us, wherever we go, has been specially tuned by the unique opportunities and challenges of being pastors in this tough post-modern society.

APPLICATION

1. Think back and acknowledge the key places that have shaped your journey so far. What happened and what did God teach you there?

2. Consider how God has located you at this moment, your country, home, place of occupation, and your church community. What is God doing in and through you by virtue of these locations? Consider both the opportunities and the difficulties of your placement. Consider how God would have you embrace His plan for your life in the context of these key places.

3. What new or different locations is God laying on your heart to explore? Are you willing to break camp and follow God to new locations as He leads you into His plan?

4. Are there any locations you may have left unadvisedly that require you to seek God again and consider returning there, being faithful to what God wanted you to do before you left?

CHAPTER 5

KEY INSIGHTS

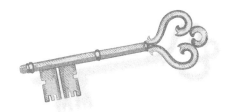

*Whenever God wants to intervene in the
affairs of the earth, He intervenes through
light, illumination, knowledge, insight,
understanding, wisdom.*

—Sunday Adelaja

Insight unravels mysteries, solves riddles, and deciphers conundrums. Many times our minds and lives feel like a tangled mess of ideas, options, and possibilities. Then suddenly a bolt of light comes into our mind and instantly everything becomes clear. Whether it's through a conversation, a book, or a sermon, these light-bulb moments are the joy of the soul. Darkness turns to light, confusion gives way to clarity and again, destiny unfolds.

INSIGHT AT THE DOCTOR'S CLINIC

From my early teenage years, I battled against a fungal disease on my skin, which would just not go away no matter what prescription I tried. There were times when my skin would clear temporarily in response to anti-fungal medication, but then after a few weeks, it would be back as strong as ever. After coming to the Lord, I prayed much about it, hoping for a miracle. Living in the UK, I noticed a slight reduction in its occurrence, but still it continued.

Finally, one day, I felt like I'd had enough. I visited our family doctor who after peering curiously at my symptoms for a few moments referred me to a skin consultant. Several weeks later, I walked into the clinic of an elderly dermatologist. After an initial examination, the doctor excused himself and walked into an adjacent room. I heard knocking sounds as he seemed to dig up a piece of equipment he may have not used for some time; when he emerged, he was bearing what looked like a purple-coloured fluorescent lamp. He plugged it into the wall socket, flicked on the switch, and shone the light on my skin.

Looking down on myself under this light, my skin looked like a zoomed-down, multi-ecological farmland of a weird plant species from an animated movie! Something about that diagnostic lamp seemed to interact with my skin and everything on it in a way that created a spectrum of diverse colours. I did not say a word, but the doctor did. 'Oh wow'! he exclaimed, his face lighting up in recognition. 'Would you mind if I brought my assistant in on this'? He did not wait for my answer and I did not mind. He returned swiftly with his colleague, and I sat there feeling like a specimen as two elderly Englishmen stared down at my body.

'Do you know what this is'? the doctor asked his colleague. The gentleman stammered out a couple of names that he quickly dismissed, then said, 'This is Pityriasis Versicolor. It is a yeast', he explained to him and me, 'and quite naturally occurring on most human skin. But for some unfortunate ones like you, it becomes a problem'.

That day I walked out of the doctor's clinic with the name of my lifelong adversary written by him on a piece of paper. He also wrote me a prescription for an ordinary shampoo that would end my decades-long battle. Many years later, I still have no trace of the skin ailment that had bothered me for decades. This story illustrates the power of a key insight.

Key Verse

When Jesus came into the region of Caesarea Philippi, He asked His disciples, saying, "Who do men say that I, the Son of Man, am?" So they said, "Some say John the Baptist, some Elijah, and others Jeremiah or one of the prophets." He said to them, "But who do you say that I am?" Simon Peter answered and said, "You are the Christ, the Son of the living God." Jesus answered and said to him, "Blessed are you, Simon Bar-Jonah, for flesh and blood has not revealed this to you, but My Father who is in heaven. And I also say to you that you are Peter, and on this rock I will build My church, and the gates of Hades shall not prevail against it. And I will give you the keys of the kingdom of heaven, and whatever you bind on earth will be bound in heaven, and whatever you loose on earth will be loosed in heaven" (Matthew 16:13-19).

At Caesarea Philippi, Jesus suddenly turns and asks His disciples a destiny-shaping question. As I am sure He expected, several answers were given in response to whom everybody was saying He is. Then Jesus raised the question to the next level, 'But who do you say that I am'? The group fell silent until Simon stepped forward, probably trembling inside as he answered, 'You are Christ...'. I have a sense Simon had never actually rehearsed, fully conceived, let alone uttered this truth before. But at this key moment, when the question was asked, everything he has observed, heard, and felt about Jesus comes together and somehow he knows that he knows.

Jesus was surprised and delighted by his answer! 'Simon Bar-Jonah', He exclaimed, 'flesh and blood has not revealed this to you...'. Peter had in this moment stepped out into the type of revelation that is the very building block of the Kingdom of God.

Earlier on as recorded in John 1:42, Jesus, upon seeing Peter for the first time, had said to him, 'You are Simon the son of Jonah. You shall be called Cephas' [Peter]. Simon must have wondered when that new name would register. And now, unexpectedly, his 'destiny name' is sounded again to him by Jesus. The key to this moment was a key insight. Jesus was saying to Peter, 'That's it, right there! That is how you step into what I have destined you to be'!

Key insights! Revelation! This ability to hear directly from Heaven is the foundation of everything God is building on earth, and the source of all the spiritual authority we need to 'forbid and permit' (bind and loose) on earth.

OTHER BIBLE VERSES ON KEY INSIGHTS

Surely the Lord God does nothing, unless He reveals His secret to His servants the prophets (Amos 3:7).

This short, powerful verse reveals that God's work on earth is always insight and revelation driven. When God's people stop listening, God stops working.

But He answered and said, "It is written, 'Man shall not live by bread alone, but by every word that proceeds from the mouth of God'" (Matthew 4:4).

Driven into the wilderness after His baptism, Jesus is set upon by the tempter in an attempt to destroy His mission and destiny. In this first temptation, the importance of revelation in a victorious believer's life has been firmly resolved. Satan disguises the temptation as the challenge to prove His Sonship by turning stone to bread. In His response, Jesus brings to the surface what the underlying seduction was. Satan was suggesting that humankind's most basic survival need is physical food. Jesus answers by revealing that in the absence of food, humans can also be supernaturally sustained by personal revelation from God.

It is important to note that this verse does not refer to every word that you read from the Bible, but rather the word of God as spoken directly by God to your heart. The original Greek word translated 'word' in this verse is the word 'rhema' and refers to a Holy Spirit-quickened insight from God. Hearing from God is the first area a believer needs to establish before battling with other areas of temptation and trials.

A PERSONAL STORY: DEBT CANCELLATION

Several years into our occupation of our leased community building, the executive pastor walked into my office with a sullen face. The process of occupying and refurbishing the community building we use was extremely expensive and necessitated much fundraising and substantial borrowing. So when we finally were able to settle down and use it for our services and programmes, we needed to slow down financially and focus on covering massive payments in addition to a quarterly substantial lease payment. But in the process of all this, it seemed like we had made a payment error somewhere.

Our accountants, as they reviewed our payments over the term of using the building had flashed out an hefty unpaid bill. They were now warning us of the need to make this huge payment, which could have also accrued months and months of interest. The payment was due immediately otherwise we could have debt collectors at our doorstep anytime. The advising accountant was putting us under great pressure, believing that this was a possible illegality on our part. Looking at the situation financially at LCF, we could not see how we could raise the amount of money needed. We needed a huge financial miracle.

One of the key gifts I have identified and sought to develop over the years in my life is the ability to know what God is saying through flash images in my mind's eye. Especially in the heat of the moment when under pressure to form an opinion or make a decision, I tend to see a flash image inwardly, and I have learnt to trust that it's always God's word for me at that moment.

Suddenly right there, sitting in my office seat, I saw a picture of Jesus in my mind's eye. Besides Him was a man in a suit whom I felt represented the payment we had to make immediately. Then I watched in my mind as Jesus pushed this man behind Him. Then the image promptly disappeared. Although I received an immediate sense of its meaning, it made no sense at all at the moment to me. I also sensed an inner voice saying: 'Do nothing about it! Leave it! Put it behind you'. And so I advised that we do exactly what I believed God had said.

Days turned to weeks, weeks to months, and months to years, and nothing happened. We then did further research about the situation. To our relief and surprise, we found that we actually had no obligation to make this large payment as advised by the accountant. It was only necessary for a particular arrangement that did not suit our contract. If we had made the payment, it would most probably have been accepted but it would not have been of any benefit for us. We would also have put our community organisation in a very difficult financial position. A key insight had saved the day and a lot of money.

There may be pressured situations that you are facing right now, and you need a key insight for the way forward. It is important for you to know and believe that God will faithfully send you the wisdom that you need before the deadlines that may be attached.

It is important to avoid getting stressed and worried about these situations and continue to affirm to yourself quietly that you will find the answer and the way forward. God will send you the key insights that you need just in time.

One of the key practices I recommend is to listen out at your waking moments. By that, I refer to what comes to mind immediately after you wake up. For others, these key insights come as they fall asleep and for others as they stand under the shower.

However they come, they key is always, peace, hope and faith that God will come through with insight and revelation.

APPLICATION

1. Think back over your life and remember the key insights that have shaped your journey so far. What did you learn and how have you stewarded the lessons?

2. Who have been the key voices in your life? Have you established the discipline of seeking insight from the people God has established as sources of insight for your life?

3. Have you cultivated a listening relationship with God? How does God typically speak to you? Do you carefully record what God is saying to you and do you act on it in obedience?

4. What areas of your life currently need key insight? Is there any specific action you can take to bring the necessary insight?

CHAPTER 6

KEY BATTLES

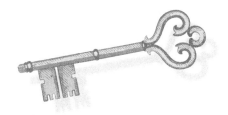

You will never be entirely comfortable. This is the truth behind the champion—he is always fighting something. To do otherwise is to settle.

—Julien Smith

Life is a battlefield. Many times the battle is brought to you with no choice of your own. At other times, it's us who should draw the battle lines and blow the war horn against the enemies we know are encroaching on our God-given territory. Some battles are optional, but others are a must, because if we ignore them or surrender in defeat without a fight, we are selling out on our destiny.

All in all, God is a Man of war and is waiting to lead us on the battlefield in taking back what belongs to us.

When Grace and I landed at Gatwick airport in August 1988, we were both granted a six-month visitor visa into the United Kingdom. As God's plan unfolded for us at our sponsoring church, Kensington Temple (KT), we knew that God was calling us to plant and lead a church in London. KT was driving an ambitious church planting programme in what was a season of visitation with thousands from the nations joining the church from all around the world.

LCF was planted in March 1991, and we surrendered our passports to a KT administrator pastor to change our visas to 'minister of religion'. After about twelve months of not hearing back from the home office, we checked with the pastor who was responsible, only to find that he had forgotten all about submitting our application to the home office. We were effectively illegal overstayers in the UK through no fault of our own. When we submitted our late application with a detailed explanation from KT about the mistake, the response was a standard one; we were ordered to leave the United Kingdom as overstayers with immediate effect and reapply for entrance from outside the UK borders.

With our firstborn son less than a year old and a very young church plant to lead and care for, we just did not know what to do. Reading up about our particular scenario as overstayers, chances were that we would not easily be granted the visas we were seeking. But we knew that God had brought us here through the prophetic word we had received about serving God abroad. We knew that if we were to get back into the UK, it was going to take a battle—a key battle.

DAVID AND GOLIATH

And a champion went out from the camp of the Philistines, named Goliath, from Gath, whose height was six cubits and a span (1 Samuel 17:4).

On the day that Goliath of Gath stood in the valley of Elah and challenged the ranks of the armies of Israel, a new chapter opened up in the story of the nation, but especially in the story of a 15-year-old boy by the name of David, the son of Jesse. This was his key moment and key battle. As God would have it, the giant Philistine defines the battle as one-on-one; not charging thousands of soldiers shouting their lungs out and swinging swords at each other.

As the story goes, no one in Israel's ranks was up to the challenge. But David had been rehearsing for this moment for years. Alone in the shepherding fields, he had faced countless one-on-one challenges from bears, lions, and the like. It was time to turn his private victories into a national one. This was his battle.

If like the rest of Israel, David had run for dear life, imagine how the Scriptures would change. Thank God that despite his size, age, and lack of war experience, he stepped out and confronted this giant, because it was his giant. Although he had the key gifts of being a harpist and psalmist, it was not going to be musicality he would use to deal with this challenge, but another honed skill. This time it was the sling and stone, a weapon that every shepherd of those days had to cultivate to deadly levels of accuracy. And so Goliath comes crashing down and the rest is history (1 Samuel 17:48-51). David's journey to kingship is suddenly accelerated as songs of his bravery are sung in the streets by those who saw or heard of his victory. If he had not stepped up to this key battle, his path to destiny would have been stalled.

As you read this, I do not doubt that you have yourself faced giants of different sizes at various times. I also know that although there is a place for family, friends, pastors, intercessors, and other supporters who have featured in your battles, there is always that moment when you have to realise that something you are going through is a battle you must take on yourself head-on! Key battles help define our identity and open doors to our destiny—but they must be fought in the mind and heart, by prayer and faith knowing God will give us the victory.

SAMSON AND THE LION

So Samson went down to Timnah with his father and mother and came to the vine-yards of Timnah. Now to his surprise, a young lion came roaring against him. And the Spirit of the Lord came mightily upon him, and he tore the lion apart as one would have torn apart a young goat, though he had nothing in his hand. But he did not tell his father or his mother what he had done (Judges 14:5-6).

Samson's conception was a miracle, fulfilling the Angel of the Lord's prophecy of his destiny as a warrior for God against the Philistines (Judges 13:2-5). He had Nazirite locks of hair showing his separation, but nothing dramatic was happening in his life at this point. Then suddenly, a lion attacks him and he tears it up with his bare hands under the power of God. This was a key battle. That day, Samson experienced for the first time what it was like for the Holy Spirit to fall upon him and transform him into a human killing machine. After that moment, he learned to trigger his gift at will, and the Philistines were to regret he was ever born!

A Personal Story: Our UK Visa Battle

I left the visa story half-told, so here is what followed. This story, besides illustrating a key battle, also illustrates almost all of the seven keys. I hope you can spot them as you read.

Having been told to leave the UK with immediate effect, my wife and I began to pray and plan our exit. The option of returning to Uganda to reapply for our return was not attractive. We could not imagine where we would stay as a family of three and where our sustenance would come from. There was nowhere else we could go—then I saw a flash vision.

As we prayed one day, in my mind's eye I saw a national flag flapping in the wind; it was blue with a yellow cross. I did not know what country that was so I looked at a flag list and found it was the nation of Sweden. There was just one person I knew in Sweden, my youth pastor in 1981 when I found Christ. We hadn't been in touch for years. Could we fly to Sweden? Could he make an arrangement to host us for a couple of weeks as we processed our reentry visa? His answer was 'Yes! Come to Gothenburg'.

The problem was that no airline ticket agent would sell us tickets as overstayers looking to fly into another European country. We would not be allowed entrance and the airline would be obliged to return us to the UK at their own expense, and with no chance of re-admission. But we kept trying other agents because of the picture I had seen. After several calls, one agent did not ask, so we bought three tickets for Gothenburg.

As only God would orchestrate, we flew in on a significant Swedish public holiday and were the last flight to arrive. As we left Heathrow Airport, our passports were unsuitably stamped and marked by a clearly upset immigration officer. Thankfully, he did not notice or challenge our exit to another European country. We prayed through the two-hour flight to Sweden and braced ourselves for what could be a hostile reception at the terminal.

When we landed, our baby son, Marvin, needed attending to, so before heading to immigration control, we found a family room and did the necessary. We then proceeded to immigration control, noting that there was no one else in sight. When we got to immigration, there was no one in sight, the airport was ghostly quiet and all the officers had left. Just as we were wondering where everybody was, we spotted a lady who seemed to be finalising locking up and we signalled for her attention. Quite astonished, she came over and asked where we were coming from. We explained that we were on the flight from London but needed to attend to the baby in the family room. She reopened her station, took our passports and paperwork, asked a couple of questions, and started to flip through my passport page by page.

My eyes were on her as she flicked through each page. As she flicked towards the page with the overstayer exit markings stamped in at Heathrow, she suddenly looked up and smiled at Marvin's little face, remarking on how cute he was. As she did her fingers flicked once more and missed the problem page. She then asked one more question and stamped a bare page for my entrance. She then took Grace's passport and began to flick through the same way. We watched and waited nervously.

Again, as if on cue, just before the troublesome page, she glanced up again at Marvin and asked something about him while her fingers flicked on. We gladly responded to her friendly remark. She then stamped Grace's passport and welcomed us to Sweden. As we walked towards the exit, we could only look at each other in wonder of what had just happened. God is the God of miracles!

Sixteen weeks after a 'battle of battles' in Sweden with the British High Commission, we flew back to London awarded with 'minister of religion' visas. Almost every day of those sixteen weeks had been tough one way or another. We stayed in the care of a Christian community that had not known us prior. We prayed, fasted, confessed, believed, and waited. The British High Commission was confused about our case, besides wondering how we had entered Sweden in the first place. Finally, after several referrals back to London and a lengthy interview, our visas were granted against all odds.

When I preached my first sermon at LCF upon return, one of the church members approached me, and while gazing steadily into my eyes, he asked, 'What happened to you out there? You are not the man who left here a few months ago'! Grace and I were not the same. We had suffered and prayed. We had stood up against an impossible situation and declared war. While in Sweden, our vision of God, ourselves, life, and the ministry had completely changed for the better. Key battles remould and reshape you as a person if you fight them in faith and prayer. As we began to minister under this new grace, LCF began to grow.

APPLICATION

1. Look back over your life and remember the key battles that have shaped your destiny so far. What happened and what did you learn?

2. What are the present battles in your life? What is being contested and what is at stake if you do not overcome? What weapons and strategies are necessary to win?

3. How would you rate yourself as a fighter? Are you prayerful, in the Word, walking by faith, thankful and persistent? Is there a need to connect yourself with prayerful people so you grow in your devotional life?

CHAPTER 7

KEY CHOICES

On every journey that you make you face choices.
At every fork in the road you make a choice.
And it is those decisions that shape our lives.

—Mike DeWine

Decisions, decisions! They must be made or nothing happens. Many times it is better to make any decision than to make none at all. 'Analysis paralysis' is the product of the fear of making mistakes and perfectionism. Many times, God will not clearly show the way, because the point in the moment is not this way or that way, but that you make a choice from the passion of your soul.

So what are you going to do about your destiny after laying this book down? The shape of your future comes back to the key choices you make today.

WORD AND SPIRIT

From the time of my conversion in March 1981, understanding and explaining the Scriptures had been my passion and driving force. But I had never imagined myself as a pastor leading a church and preaching regularly. So when the call to plant LCF came, I had to make several adjustments in my heart and mind. Part of my battle was dealing with a remnant sense of social awkwardness that I had always felt from childhood, in addition to the challenge of having to learn on the job. In the first few months of preaching, teaching, and ministry, I settled down into a way of doing things. Our services were timely, orderly, and quite predictable.

A couple of weeks before our launch, another church led by a fellow Ugandan had just launched in Charlton, South London. When LCF was birthed, some in our fairly small immigrant community were attending both churches and watching to see the uniqueness of these two church families. Then a comment by one of our attendees was brought to my attention: 'If you want the

Word you go to LCF...but if you want power you go to the other church'.

This remark broke my heart. Having been converted in an environment of power, signs and wonders, and out-pourings of the Holy Spirit, I knew what it was like to minister in power. But I realised that over the ten years since my salvation I had pursued the stewardship of the Word more than that of the Spirit. Also, I and many like me had by this time realised that most power-focused churches had developed a reputation for being shallow in the Word, besides other aspects that were associated with gimmickry and bad practice. On our side as teaching churches, there was laxity in the pursuit of the power gifts of the Holy Spirit.

Now as a pastor in a highly needy immigrant community, I was being faced with a situation where I had to make a decision. LCF had to be a church that faithfully stewards both the Word and the Spirit of God.

From that day, I began a journey of personal trans-formation, which was mainly climaxed during the six-teen weeks in Sweden as narrated in the previous chapter. While waiting there for our visas to be issued, I had a major encounter with the Lord. In the wee hours of the night, sitting on the lounge floor in the darkness, staring at a spot of light reflecting off a metallic frame on the wall, I made a choice in response to the Lord to return to London as a revivalist.

Much of our time in Sweden, my wife and I devoted myself to meditation and prayer to unlock and flow in the power gifts of the Holy Spirit. Upon return to the UK, the difference in ministry focus was clear. Our prophetic gifts became more clearly expressed and outpourings of God's power became more frequent. Now, no one needed to choose between the two churches—at LCF people would encounter both Word and Spirit.

DEFIANCE LED TO DELIVERANCE

By faith Moses, when he was born, was hidden three months by his parents, because they saw he was a beautiful child; and they were not afraid of the king's command. By faith Moses, when he became of age, refused to be called the son of Pharaoh's daughter, choosing rather to suffer affliction with the people of God than to enjoy the passing pleasures of sin, esteeming the reproach of Christ greater riches than the treasures in Egypt; for he looked to the reward. By faith he forsook Egypt, not fearing the wrath of the king; for he endured as seeing Him who is invisible (Hebrews 11:23-27).

The deliverance of Israel from the bondage of Egypt was promised by God to Abraham way before the nation was even formed. God said that they would be in captivity for 400 years before they would be set free (Genesis 15:13-14). When the moment of this deliverance arrived, it unfolded humanly through key people making key choices. Moses' mother made an extraordinary choice not to be afraid and defied the order of Pharaoh. While every Hebrew woman surrendered their sons to the sword, she hid Moses and floated him down the Nile River in a basket made of bulrushes. This decision alone by a passionate, resolute mother set into motion a cascade of events that led to the deliverance of a whole nation.

In the same spirit of defiant decision making, Moses, when he was of age, made a dramatic decision to walk away from the pomp and privilege of being a prince of Egypt to associate with his enslaved people. His decision was costly and dangerous, but the loss he suffered in status put him on a trajectory to fulfil God's will for his life.

Everyone comes to these key moments when key choices need to be made in favour of our God-given destinies. Many times the price is high and those around us may question our very sanity. Whether it affects relationships, careers, finances, or else, the price must be counted and the decision made for Christ.

OTHER BIBLE VERSES ON KEY CHOICES

- ## *Elijah's Challenge to Israel*

Elijah came to all the people, and said, "How long will you falter between two opinions? If the Lord is God, follow Him; but if Baal, follow him." But the people answered him not a word (1 Kings 18:21).

At a pivotal point in Israel, Elijah challenges the nation to make a choice concerning who they are to worship. Wavering between two opinions was just not going to do. We too need to make critical choices about our devotion to God. Lukewarm, half-hearted Christianity is destroying the witness of the Church worldwide. Now like never before, the church must choose to worship and serve God with all our hearts.

As I write these lines, the world is in the grip of a global viral pandemic. Nations are on lockdown, economies in meltdown, and thousands of people are dying daily. All around the world, choices and decisions are being made for better and for worse. What choices does God need you to make in line with His purposes on earth today?

- ## *The Church Decides to Pray*

Peter was therefore kept in prison, but constant prayer was offered to God for him by the church.

And when Herod was about to bring him out, that night Peter was sleeping, bound with two chains between two soldiers, and the guards before the door were keeping the prison. Now behold, an angel of the Lord stood by him, and a light shone in the prison; and he struck Peter on the side and raised him up, saying, "Arise quickly!" And his chains fell off his hands (Acts 12:5-7).

In the first few verses of Acts chapter 12, Herod arrests and kills James who was the pastor of the church in Jerusalem. The event would have been heart-wrenching for the body of believers. What disturbs me most is that this account, the murder of this great man who was one of the three in Jesus' inner circle, is recorded in a single verse. The story quickly moves on and I am screaming, 'Wait! Herod just killed James the greater, the brother of John'!

This huge loss to the church can only be tolerated by what followed next! When Herod saw that James' murder pleased the Jews, he then arrested Peter with the same murderous agenda, but the church made a decision to pray.

Before the murder of James, the church could easily have thought it impossible for such a giant of the faith to be killed by Herod. When he was, the church sat up in attention. They realised God's will does not just happen on earth. There has to be a passionate arising to prayer and intercession by the church. So when Peter was arrested, a campaign of constant prayer was mobilised on his behalf. This decision to separate themselves in extended prayer turned the outcome around and an angel was sent from Heaven to release Peter from prison.

I shiver at the thought of what would have become of the early church and its witness if the church had not made this radical choice to pray.

What choices are you making today concerning your life, family, career or ministry?

APPLICATION

1. Look back over your life and take note of key choices that have shaped your destiny so far. What choices did you make and what were the outcomes?

2. What regrettable choices have you made in the past and what were the consequences? How has God's grace reworked in your life to turn these consequences around for His glory?

3. What key choices are you facing currently? Are you committed to pay the price and make the sacrifices necessary for the choices that lead you in God's given path?

4. Are there are key decisions that you have been putting off because of fear or self-preservation? Are you now ready to make the change?

AFTERWORD

POST COVID-19 CHOICES

As I bring this book to a close, I wish to share my heart about where we are as the body of Christ amid unprecedented global events. Some reading this book may not have been born or old enough to have experienced the Corona Virus epidemic that ravaged our world from the year 2020 leaving thousands dead in its wake. As I write this, the global death toll is reaching 820,000 people, with concerns of a second wave of infections and re-infections in previously unlocked countries.

A few weeks ago, I conducted the funeral of a pastor who passed away from Covid-19. You will remember that I testified about this pastor in the Key Battles chapter as he hosted my family in Sweden. He had other underlying conditions that contributed to his rapid decline in health. He has ascended to glory and we celebrate his legacy of prayer and revival leadership.

Also as I write this, a friend who was fighting for his life on ventilation in intensive care is now back at home with his family after doctors had declared him past the point of recovery. It took an extraordinary feat of extended prayer and persistent faith by the church community to witness his sudden turn around to recovery. It is in many ways a modern tale akin to the prayer that set Peter free from prison as recounted above. Last night I heard of the passing of a couple, husband and wife, who both passed away in their 60s in hospital. They contracted the infection and died a few days apart away from each other. Their relatives are perplexed and in lockdown, unable to do much at the moment as the most immediate relatives are in the same age bracket with underlying conditions, which makes them extremely vulnerable.

Our world has changed. We—the Church—cannot remain the same.

Choices need to be made not tomorrow but now. I have made some really intense decisions to match the season we have entered. At the heart of my choices is an even more radical separation to God and His purposes on earth. Through the lens of our current suffering and the devotion it has created in me, I see a completely different church. I want to be signed up by the Lord for the highest possible manifestations of the glory of God on earth. Lukewarm Christianity is not enough. We must choose to turn to God afresh, choose to pray and seek His face like never before. The world needs us—the sick, the dying, the bereaved, those who have lost their livelihoods.

Also, the signs of the times are upon us. The Lord's return is near. May we prepare ourselves for Him and bring many into His loving embrace. This is the time to embrace God's call for your life and set your eyes on his destiny for your life!

Apply the seven keys in this book passionately in your life. Set your eyes on everything that God declares you to be. And may God bless, keep and use you mightily in these most extraordinary times. Amen!

ABOUT THE AUTHOR

Pastor Lincoln and Grace Serwanga are the senior pastors at LCF. Through their faithful ministry LCF has grown to become the thriving church that it is today. From the onset of their ministry, they have been driven by a passion to see God do something special around the world in revival. This passion is the driving force behind their revelatory preaching and forms the core of the radical vision and identity of the church. Lincoln also runs Equus Discipleship, a ground-breaking, online programme that helps break stagnation and kick-start spiritual growth.

Contact Information

Address: 9-11 Cottage Green,
Camberwell, London, UK SE5 7ST

Phone: 020 770 86931

https://www.mylcfchurch.com/
https:/www.lincolnserwanga.com

www.facebook.com/LibertyLondonLCF/

Get in touch with us:
EAGLE'S WINGS INTERNATIONAL

PO Box 6295, McKinney TX 75071, USA
Email: office@e-wings.net

Printed in Great Britain
by Amazon